4-Step
Soup Recipes

Sterling Publishing Co., Inc.
New York

D1472596

Library of Congress Cataloging-in-Publication Data Available

10   9   8   7   6   5   4   3   2

Published by Sterling Publishing Co., Inc.
387 Park Avenue South, New York, NY 10016
Originally published in Canada in 2002 by
Éditions TOTAL Publishing under the title *4 Steps Soup Recipes*
© 2002 by Éditions TOTAL Publishing

Sterling ISBN 1-4027-0731-2

Contents

Introduction   **5**

Chilled soups   **7**

Hearty soups   **21**

Cream Soups   **67**

Traditional Soups   **141**

Dessert Soups   **173**

Index   **186**

Introduction

Nowadays, eating well isn't as easy as one would think. Our overloaded schedules leave us little time for cooking. We are eating more and more frozen, tasteless, prepackaged meals than ever before, or else we choose fast food restaurants, which do not serve very well-balanced meals. We also lack inspiration when it comes to planning and varying our menus.

With its modern and dynamic approach, the **4-Step Cooking Collection** offers welcome solutions on how to quickly prepare dishes that are both tasty and nourishing. Come and discover the joys of healthy eating with every turn of the page. The recipes presented in this collection are easy to prepare. Each recipe is broken down into 4 easy steps, no more, no less. What's more, most of these recipes use ingredients that you will find in your local grocery store, thus helping you to save unnecessary time running around. Now eating well is as easy as 1-2-3… 4! Good ingredients, clear and precise instructions, a few "culinary secrets," that's all you need to surprise your guests. You are never more than 4 steps away from your next delicious meal!

Soup is nourishing and comforting, and is a wonderful opening to a meal. Some of the heartier soups can even be served as the main course. Commercial versions of soup never fail to conjure up visions of a thin, tasteless liquid that contains unrecognizable little ingredients. But, in reality, the large family of soups is much more diversified, surprising and appetizing than that which the food industry offers us in the form of cans or dehydrated packages.

With the 4-step recipes contained in this book, you will soon realize that you can prepare delicious soup in just about the same amount of time it takes to find and open a can.

Soup is anything but monotonous. It can be prepared with almost any ingredient: meat, poultry, fish or vegetables. Just add a few herbs, spices and various other seasonings. Given its limitless possibilities, you will be able to add to your menus and take advantage of the benefits of this legendary broth. No wonder you'll be wanting to create soups more often. That's why there is such diversity among all the recipes presented here, with one important exception—no matter what the soup, yours will be ready in just 4 steps!

Yogurt and Crisp Vegetable Soup

4 to 6 SERVINGS

3 cups	plain yogurt
1½ cups	tomato juice
	juice of 1 lemon
½	English cucumber, peeled and finely chopped
1	yellow pepper, chopped
1	bunch of green onions, sliced thinly
	paprika, to taste
	hot sauce (Tabasco or other), to taste
	salt and freshly ground pepper, to taste

1 In a large bowl, blend the yogurt together with the tomato juice and lemon juice.

2 Add half of the chopped vegetables.

3 Season to taste with paprika, hot sauce and salt and pepper. Cover and refrigerate for 2 to 3 hours to blend the flavors.

4 Taste for seasoning. When serving, pour the soup into bowls and garnish with the remaining chopped vegetables.

Note

If you want to make this soup a full-course meal, all you have to do is add some cooked fish or small shrimp. Accompany with crusty bread and a small green salad.

Chilled soups

Chilled Cauliflower Velouté

4 SERVINGS

6 cups	chicken broth
4 cups	cauliflower florets
2	green onions, sliced thinly
	salt and freshly ground pepper, to taste
1 cup	plain yogurt
	fresh mixed herbs, chopped, to taste

1 In a large covered saucepan, bring the broth to boil over high heat. Add the cauliflower and the green onions. Lower the heat, cover and cook for 5 minutes or until the cauliflower is tender.

2 Purée the soup in batches in a food processor. Transfer to a large bowl. Season to taste with salt and pepper.

3 Cover and refrigerate the soup for several hours, until cold.

4 Just before serving, whisk in the yogurt and garnish with a pinch of fresh mixed herbs.

Note

A good way to clean cauliflower is to soak it head down for 15 minutes in cold water to which salt and vinegar have been added.

Chilled soups

Chilled Melon Soup

4 SERVINGS

2	ripe cantaloupes, cut in half and seeded
¼ cup	plain yogurt
¼ cup	chicken broth
1 tbsp	fresh mint leaves
	grated zest and juice of 1 lemon (use zest for garnish)
	salt and freshly ground pepper, to taste
	plain yogurt (garnish)
	mint sprigs (garnish)

1 Remove the pulp from the cantaloupe halves using a spoon, reserving the rinds. Wrap them and refrigerate to use as bowls.

2 Purée the cantaloupes in a food processor. Add the yogurt, chicken broth, mint leaves, and lemon juice, and process until very smooth.

3 Transfer to a large bowl. Season with salt and pepper. Cover and refrigerate for 2 to 3 hours, until cold.

4 Cut a thin slice of the bottom of each melon rind so it sits flat and place in soup plates. Serve the soup in the melon "bowls." Garnish with a spoonful of yogurt, the lemon zest and mint sprigs.

Chilled soups

Chilled Yogurt and Fennel Soup

4 SERVINGS

4 cups	chicken broth
¼ cup	minute rice
	salt and freshly ground pepper, to taste
2 tbsp	finely chopped fresh fennel
1 cup	plain yogurt
1 tbsp	finely chopped fresh parsley

1 Bring the chicken broth to a boil in a medium saucepan over high heat.

2 Add the rice. Season with salt and pepper, lower the heat, cover and let simmer for 5 minutes, until the rice is tender.

3 Remove the saucepan from the heat and add the fennel to the hot soup. Cool in the refrigerator for several hours.

4 When serving, whisk in the yogurt and taste for seasoning. Ladle into very cold bowls and garnish with the parsley.

Note
Soups that are served chilled must be tasted for seasoning both when hot and later when cooled, in order to properly adjust seasoning.

Chilled soups

Chilled Algerian Soup

4 SERVINGS

4 cups	chicken broth
½ lb	pastrami, cut in thin slices
¼ cup	minute rice
2	egg yolks, beaten
1 cup	plain yogurt
1 tbsp	chopped fresh mint
2 tbsp	chopped fresh parsley
	freshly ground pepper, to taste
4	sprigs of fresh mint and parsley (garnish)

1 In a large heavy saucepan, combine the chicken broth and the pastrami. Bring to a boil over high heat. Add the rice, lower the heat, cover and simmer for 5 minutes until the rice is tender.

2 In a small bowl, whisk the egg yolks with a little of the hot soup to warm them, then transfer to the soup, whisking well. Remove from the heat. Transfer to a large bowl. Cover and refrigerate for 2 to 3 hours until cold.

3 Purée the soup in batches in a food processor. Return to the bowl. Whisk in the yogurt, parsley and mint. Season to taste with pepper, if needed.

4 Ladle into soup bowls and garnish each with a sprig of mint and parsley. Serve well chilled.

Note
This soup will be delicious accompanied with toasted strips of pita bread.

Chilled soups

Gazpacho

6 to 8 SERVINGS

1	English cucumber, peeled and cut in chunks
1	green pepper, halved and seeded
1	small onion, quartered
1	celery stalk, cut in chunks
1	garlic clove, peeled
2⅓ cups	crushed canned tomatoes
1 cup	tomato juice or vegetable juice
	salt and freshly ground pepper, to taste
	hot sauce (Tabasco or other), to taste
	pinch of sugar
4	lemon wedges (garnish)
4	parsley sprigs (garnish)

1 Finely chop each vegetable separately using a food processor. Place all the chopped vegetables in a large bowl.

2 Add the crushed tomatoes and the juice. Mix well to a smooth consistency.

3 Season to taste with salt and pepper. Add the hot sauce and the sugar. Cover and refrigerate for 2 to 3 hours, until ready to serve.

4 Check the soup's consistency, thinning with a bit of tomato juice as required. Taste for seasoning. Ladle into bowls and garnish each with a lemon wedge and a sprig of fresh parsley.

Chilled soups

Chilled Avocado Soup

6 SERVINGS

3 cups	chicken broth
1 cup	light cream
½ tsp	freshly ground pepper
2	ripe avocados, well ripened
½ cup	dry white wine
	juice of 1 lemon
	salt and freshly ground pepper, to taste

1 In a heavy medium saucepan, bring the chicken broth, cream and pepper to a boil, over medium heat, stirring well.

2 Cut the avocados in half, remove the pit and the peel and cut into cubes.

3 Add the avocados, wine and lemon juice to the broth; cook for 5 to 7 minutes, stirring often, until just heated through.

4 Purée the soup in batches in a food processor. Season with salt and pepper. Cover and refrigerate for 2 to 3 hours, until cold. Taste for seasoning and serve.

Note
The avocado must be cooked with care, because if heated too long, it quickly loses its flavor. This soup should be eaten the same day as it is made.

Chilled soups

Pistou

4 SERVINGS

6 cups	chicken broth
¾ cup	each cubed carrots, celery, leeks
¾ cup	cut green beans,(1 in. pieces)
1	small onion, chopped
	salt and freshly ground pepper, to taste
¼ cup	fresh basil, chopped (approximately 12 leaves)
2	garlic cloves, sliced thinly
1 tbsp	olive oil
2	peeled tomatoes, seeded and cubed (garnish)
	grated parmesan cheese, to taste (optional)

1 In a large saucepan, bring the chicken broth to a boil over high heat.

2 Add the vegetables, lower the heat, cover and cook for approximately 20 minutes, or until tender. Season with salt and pepper.

3 Purée the basil, garlic, olive oil and a bit of the hot soup in a food processor. Transfer to a small bowl.

4 Ladle the hot soup into bowls and garnish with a bit of the basil mixture, the tomato cubes and grated cheese, if using.

Hearty soups

Spinach and Lentil Soup

4 SERVINGS

4 cups	chicken broth or vegetable broth
2 cups	diced canned tomatoes, with juice
1 can	lentils, drained
2 cups	cooked lentils
2	celery stalks, chopped
2	onions, sliced thinly
1	carrot, grated
2	garlic cloves, sliced thinly
1 pack	fresh spinach, chopped
1 tbsp	lemon juice
	salt and freshly ground pepper, to taste

Garnish

¼ cup	grated white cheddar cheese
1 tsp	curry powder
4	slices crusty bread, toasted

1 In a large heavy saucepan, bring the broth, tomatoes, lentils, celery, onions, carrot and garlic to a boil over medium heat. Lower the heat, cover and let simmer for 5 minutes.

2 Add the spinach, cover and simmer for 4 minutes, until all the vegetables are tender.

3 Add the lemon juice and season to taste with salt and pepper.

4 Serve the soup in bowls with the cheese toasts. Top each toast with grated cheese and a sprinkle of curry powder.

Note

Dry lentils do not have to be soaked before cooking. You can purée this soup in a food processor, making it an excellent creamed soup.

Hearty soups

Chick Pea Surprise

4 to 6 SERVINGS

1 tbsp	butter
1 cup	chopped onion
1 cup	diced celery
1 cup	thinly sliced leek
6 cups	chicken broth
1 can	chick peas, drained
1½ cups	sliced mushrooms
	salt and freshly ground pepper, to taste
1 cup	shredded fresh spinach
1 tbsp	chopped fresh cilantro
2 tbsp	chopped fresh chives (optional)
2	fresh bread slices, toasted and cut into triangles

1 In a large heavy saucepan, melt the butter over medium heat. Add the onion, celery and the leek and cook, stirring often, until tender.

2 Add the chicken broth. Bring to a boil. Lower the heat and let simmer for 10 minutes.

3 Add the chick peas and the mushrooms, let simmer another 5 minutes. Season with salt and pepper.

4 Just before serving, stir in the spinach, chives and cilantro. Ladle into bowls and serve with the toast triangles.

Hearty soups

Beef and Cabbage Soup

4 SERVINGS

1 tsp	vegetable oil or olive oil
1 lb	round steak, trimmed and cut into cubes
½ cup	chopped onion
½ tsp	minced garlic
	salt and freshly ground pepper, to taste
6 cups	water
1 cup	tomato juice
¾ cup	cubed carrots
¾ cup	cubed celery
¾ cup	cubed peeled potato
½ cup	shredded cabbage
⅓ cup	long-grain rice
1	bouquet garni (1 bay leaf, 1 sprig of thyme, 1 sprig of parsley)
1 can (15 oz)	chick peas, drained
2 tbsp	chopped fresh parsley (garnish)

1 Heat the oil in a large heavy saucepan over medium heat. Sauté the cubed beef for 5 minutes, until browned. Add the onion and garlic and season with salt and pepper.

2 Add the water and the tomato juice and bring to a boil. Lower the heat, cover and simmer for 30 minutes.

3 Add the carrots, celery, potato, cabbage, rice and the bouquet garni; let simmer covered for another 30 minutes, until the beef, rice and the vegetables are very tender.

4 Add the chick peas and heat through. Serve generous portions in large soup bowls; garnish with the chopped parsley.

Note

To make a bouquet garni, wrap the bay leaf, thyme and parsley in a small square of cheesecoth. Tie securely with kitchen string, leaving the ends of the string long. Remove the bouquet garni when the soup has cooked.

Hearty soups

Soup Royale

8 SERVINGS

8 cups	beef broth
½ cup	dry sherry
2 cups	julienne-cut ham
2 cups	shredded cooked chicken
	salt and freshly ground pepper, to taste
2	hard-cooked eggs, finely chopped
2 cups	croutons
4	parsley springs (garnish)

1 Pour the beef broth into a large saucepan.

2 Add the sherry and bring to a boil over high heat. Lower the heat so the broth is simmering.

3 Add the strips of ham and chicken; simmer for 5 minutes and season to taste with salt and pepper.

4 Stirring slowly, add the eggs and the croutons. Ladle into soup bowls. Garnish each bowl with a parsley sprig.

Soupe à la Bonne Femme

6 SERVINGS

1 tbsp	butter
1	chopped garlic clove
½ cup	chopped celery leaves
½ cup	chopped celery
2	white parts of leeks, thinly sliced
2	potatoes, peeled and cut into small cubes
1	turnip, peeled and diced
1	cucumber, peeled, seeded and cut into pieces
8 cups	vegetable broth
	celery salt, to taste
	fresh ground pepper, to taste
1 cup	frozen green peas
2	bread slices, cut into small cubes
1 tbsp	melted butter
1 tbsp	finely chopped fresh chives

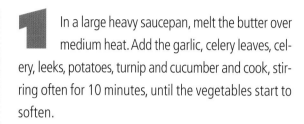

1 In a large heavy saucepan, melt the butter over medium heat. Add the garlic, celery leaves, celery, leeks, potatoes, turnip and cucumber and cook, stirring often for 10 minutes, until the vegetables start to soften.

2 Add the vegetable broth; season with the celery salt and pepper. Bring to a boil. Lower the heat, cover and cook for 25 minutes. Add the peas and continue cooking for another 10 minutes, until the vegetables are very tender.

3 Meanwhile, preheat the oven to 300°F. Mix the bread cubes, melted butter and chives in a bowl. Place on a baking sheet and bake for approximately 15 minutes, turning once or twice, until browned and crisp.

4 Ladle the soup into preheated bowls, garnish with the croutons and serve piping hot.

Hearty soups

Chicken Rice Soup

2 SERVINGS

1 can	condensed chicken broth
1 cup	water
¼ cup	long-grain rice
¼ cup	finely chopped green onions
3 tbsp	butter
⅓ cup	all-purpose flour
¼ tsp	dried sage
	salt and freshly ground pepper, to taste
1 cup	light cream
¾ cup	cubed cooked chicken or turkey
2	slices of crisp-cooked bacon, crumbled
2 tbsp	chopped green pepper
2 tbsp	dry sherry (optional)

1 In a heavy medium saucepan, mix the chicken broth and water. Add the rice and green onions. Bring to a boil over high heat. Lower the heat, cover and let simmer for 20 to 30 minutes or until the rice is tender.

2 In a heavy medium skillet, melt the butter over medium heat. Stir in the flour and sage; season with salt and pepper. Cook for 1 minute, stirring constantly. Gradually add the cream, stirring constantly, until the mixture thickens and boils.

3 Slowly add the cream sauce to the rice mixture while stirring. Add the remaining ingredients. Heat slowly, stirring often; do not boil.

4 Taste for seasoning. Ladle into bowls, garnish with croutons and serve immediately.

Hearty soups

Italian Vegetable Soup (Minestrone)

4 SERVINGS

1 tbsp	vegetable oil
½ cup	thinly sliced leek
1	thinly sliced small onion
½ cup	cubed celery
½ cup	cubed carrots
6 cups	chicken broth
	salt and freshly ground pepper, to taste
12	meat- or cheese-filled tortellini
1	egg, beaten
2 tbsp	chopped fresh parsley
2 tbsp	chopped fresh basil
1 tbsp	freshly grated parmesan cheese (garnish)
4	bread slices, toasted and cut into triangles

1 Heat the oil in a large heavy saucepan over low heat. Add the leek, onion, celery and carrots and cook gently for approximately 4 minutes, until the vegetables start to soften.

2 Add the chicken broth, and increase the heat and bring to a boil. Lower the heat and let simmer for 15 minutes. Season to taste with salt and pepper.

3 Add the tortellini and let simmer another 10 minutes, until tender. In a bowl, whisk the egg with a little of the hot soup to warm it, then transfer to the soup, stirring constantly. Remove from the heat.

4 Add the parsley and the basil. Ladle into bowls and serve with freshly grated parmesan and the toasted bread triangles.

Hearty soups

Exotic Broccoli Soup

4 to 6 SERVINGS

Home-made chicken stock

8 cups	water
1 lb	chicken bones
1	small onion, quartered
1	celery stalk, cut in chunks
1	bunch of parsley
1	bay leaf
	salt and freshly ground pepper, to taste

1 tbsp	vegetable oil
½ cup	cubed celery
½ cup	chopped onion
1 cup	shredded Chinese cabbage
1 cup	small broccoli florets, blanched
1 cup	drained canned sliced hearts of palm
1	lime, cut in decorative slices
2 tbsp	chopped fresh cilantro

1 Bring the water to a boil in a large saucepan over high heat. Add the chicken bones, onion, celery, parsley and the bay leaf. Season with salt and pepper. Lower the heat and let simmer for 20 minutes; strain and reserve the liquid.

2 In another large saucepan, heat the oil over medium heat. Add the celery, Chinese cabbage, onion and cook, stirring often until tender.

3 Add the chicken stock and bring to a boil. Lower the heat and let simmer for 15 minutes.

4 Add the broccoli florets, the hearts of palm, the lime slices and the cilantro. Heat slowly, taste for seasoning and serve.

Note

Chinese or napa cabbage has an elongated form that resembles both celery and romaine lettuce. Excellent in soups, it can be sautéed or poached, and serve as an accompaniment to meats or fish.

Fresh cilantro is sometimes difficult to locate. You can replace it with fresh celery leaves or parsley.

Hearty soups

Vegetable Rice Soup

6 to 8 SERVINGS

1 tbsp	vegetable oil
1	onion, finely chopped
2	carrots, peeled and thinly sliced
2	white turnips, peeled and cubed
½	rutabaga, peeled and cubed
1	garlic clove, crushed through a press
¼ cup	tomato paste
7 cups	vegetable broth
2	potatoes, peeled and cubed
⅓ cup	cubed tomatoes
⅓ cup	cooked white rice
⅓ cup	frozen cut green beans
1 tsp	chopped fresh parsley
	salt and freshly ground pepper, to taste

1 In a large heavy saucepan, heat the oil over low heat. Add the onion and cook for 5 minutes. Add the carrots, turnips and rutabaga, increase the heat to medium and cook, stirring often, for another 5 minutes.

2 Add the tomato paste and garlic. Mix well to coat the vegetables.

3 Stir in the vegetable broth and the potatoes and bring to a boil. Lower the heat and let simmer for 20 minutes, until the vegetables are tender.

4 Add the tomato cubes, rice, green beans and the parsley. Season to taste with salt and pepper and heat through. Serve piping hot.

Note
Potatoes can be peeled and cubed in advance if you soak them in cold water, to stop them from discolouring.
Vegetables will cook more evenly if they are cut to the same size.
The addition of canned beans or chunks of cooked meat makes this dish a complete meal.

Hearty soups

Julienned Vegetable
and Vermicelli Bouillon

4 SERVINGS

1	carrot, peeled
1/2 cup	snow-peas, stringed
1	white part of leek
1 wedge	cabbage
1	red pepper
6 cups	chicken broth
4 oz	vermicelli pasta
1 cup	mung bean sprouts (optional)
	salt and freshly ground pepper, to taste

1 Cut all the vegetables into julienne strips (very thin sticks).

2 Bring the chicken broth to a boil in a large saucepan over high heat.

3 To the broth, add the following ingredients in order: carrot, snow peas, vermicelli, leek, cabbage, bean sprouts (if using) and red pepper; bring to a boil. Season to taste with salt and pepper.

4 Remove from the heat, cover and let stand for 10 minutes, until the vermicelli is al denté. Serve in bowls or in a soup tureen.

Hearty soups

Classic Clam Chowder

4 SERVINGS

1 tbsp	butter
2	potatoes, peeled and cubed
2	carrots, chopped
1	onion, chopped
1 can (10 oz)	whole clams, with juice
1 cup	water
2 cups	milk
	salt and freshly ground pepper, to taste

1 In a large heavy saucepan, melt the butter over medium heat. Add the vegetables and cook, stirring often, for 5 minutes until lightly browned.

2 Add the clams and their juice, and enough water to cover all the ingredients. Bring to a boil. Lower the heat and let simmer until the vegetables are tender and the liquid is reduced by half, about 15 minutes.

3 Pour the milk into the saucepan and heat, stirring constantly. Do not let boil. As soon as bubbles form, lower the heat and let simmer for 3 to 4 minutes, until the flavors have blended.

4 Season generously with salt and pepper. Serve with whole wheat crackers.

Note

Mussels, oysters or shrimp may be used in place of clams. If you use fresh or frozen seafood instead of canned, add ½ cup of clambroth or fish stock when adding the seafood.

Hearty soups

Fiesta Chicken Soup

4 SERVINGS

2 cups	cubed cooked chicken
6 cups	chicken broth
½ tsp	celery seeds
½ tsp	coarse-ground black pepper
2	garlic cloves, sliced thinly
1 can (28 oz)	tomatoes, drained and cubed
1	green pepper, cut into cubes
1	onion, chopped
2 tbsp	chopped fresh cilantro or parsley
½ tsp	ground cumin
½ tsp	crushed red pepper
	salt to taste
1¼ cups	frozen or drained canned corn niblets
4	green onions, sliced thinly
1 cup	cooked white rice

Garnish

2 tbsp	chopped fresh parsley
	corn chips
1 cup	grated white cheddar cheese

1 In a large heavy saucepan, combine the chicken, the broth, garlic, celery seeds and black pepper. Bring to a boil over high heat. Lower the heat, cover and let simmer for 30 minutes.

2 Add the tomatoes, green pepper, onion, cilantro or parsley, cumin and the crushed red pepper. Season with salt and let simmer for 10 minutes, until the vegetables are tender.

3 Add the corn, green onions and the rice. Cook until the soup boils and the corn is tender. Remove from the heat.

4 Ladle the soup into ovenproof bowls, and garnish with the cheddar and chopped parsley. Melt the cheese under the broiler, if desired. Serve with corn chips.

Hearty soups

Ham and Lentil Soup

4 to 6 SERVINGS

2 tbsp	butter
1 cup	peeled cubed butternut squash
¾ cup	thinly sliced leek
¾ cup	sliced celery
½ cup	cubed carrot
½ cup	chopped onions
1 cup	lentils, softened and rinsed
2	tomatoes, seeded and cubed
½ cup	cubed ham
2 tbsp	chopped fresh parsley
½ tsp	minced garlic
6 cups	chicken broth
1 cup	milk
½ cup	cubed firm tofu
	salt and freshly ground pepper to taste

1 In a large heavy saucepan, melt the butter over medium heat. Add the celery, carrots, leek, squash and onion and cook, stirring often, for 10 minutes, until the vegetables start to soften.

2 Stir in the lentils, tomatoes, ham, parsley and garlic.

3 Add the chicken broth and bring to a boil. Lower the heat, cover and let simmer for 35 to 40 minutes.

4 Stir in the milk and the tofu and heat through. Season with salt and pepper. Serve piping hot in deep soup bowls.

Note
If you wish, replace the ham with chicken or smoked turkey.

Hearty soups

Gruyère Soup

4 SERVINGS

2 tbsp	butter
1	small onion, finely chopped
2 tbsp	all-purpose flour
1 cup	beef broth
2 cups	milk
1 cup	grated gruyère cheese
½ cup	cubed ham or cooked sausage
	salt and freshly ground pepper, to taste
	paprika, to taste
	small bread croutons (garnish)

1 In a medium microwave dish or casserole, melt the butter on medium power. Add the onion and microwave on medium for 1 minute.

2 Sprinkle with the flour, and stir in the beef broth and milk. Microwave on high for 10 minutes, stirring once or twice, until bubbly and slightly thickened.

3 Remove from the microwave. Add the grated cheese, stir until the cheese has completely melted, then add the ham or sausage.

4 Season with salt and pepper and serve sprinkled with paprika and garnished with croutons.

Note
The cheese must be cooked over low heat for a short time only to avoid it becoming rubbery in texture.

Vegetable Soup

4 SERVINGS

4 tbsp	butter
1	onion, chopped
2	garlic cloves, chopped
2	celery stalks, sliced thinly
2	carrots, peeled and cubed
½	rutabaga, peeled and cubed
1	potato, peeled and cubed
1 cup	sliced cabbage
	salt and freshly ground pepper, to taste
1	bay leaf
1 tsp	dried oregano
1 tsp	dried thyme
2 cups	beef broth
1 can (16 oz)	diced tomatoes, drained
½ cup	short pasta

1 In a large heavy saucepan, melt the butter over medium heat. Add the onion and garlic, and cook, stirring often, until tender.

2 Add the remaining vegetables, and cook, stirring often, for 5 to 10 minutes, until slightly softened. Season with salt and pepper and add the herbs.

3 Add the beef broth and the tomatoes, increase the heat and bring to a boil. Add the pasta and cook for 5 to 8 minutes, until the vegetables and pasta are tender.

4 Taste for seasoning and remove the bay leaf. Serve immediately to avoid overcooking the pasta.

Hearty soups

Floating Avocado Soup

4 SERVINGS

½ lb	skinned and boned chicken breast halves, cut in julienne strips
4 cups	chicken broth
1	chile pepper, seeded and finely chopped
4	garlic cloves, minced
	salt and freshly ground pepper, to taste
1	ripe avocado, halved peeled, pitted and cut in slices
¼ cup	finely chopped fresh cilantro or parsley,

1 In a medium saucepan, bring the chicken strips and the broth to a boil over medium-high heat. Lower the heat and simmer for 5 minutes.

2 Add the chile pepper and garlic and season to taste with salt and pepper. Let simmer for 8 minutes.

3 Place the avocado slices one at a time in the hot soup.

4 When the avocado slices float to the surface, the soup is ready to serve in bowls. Garnish with the cilantro or parsley.

Hearty soups

Cream of Leek
and Smoked Oysters

4 SERVINGS

2 cups	fish or seafood stock
¾ cup	dry white wine
2	white parts of leeks, sliced thinly
4	potatoes, peeled and cut into ½ in cubes
1 tbsp	fresh thyme leaves or
1 tsp	dried thyme
	salt and freshly ground pepper, to taste
1½ cups	milk
1 tbsp	cornstarch, mixed with 2 tbsp cold water
2 cans (10 oz)	smoked oysters, drained
1	red pepper, cut into ¼ in cubes
2 tbsp	chopped fresh parsley

1 In a large heavy saucepan, bring the stock and the wine to a boil over high heat.

2 Add the potatoes and the leeks. Lower the heat, cover and simmer for 20 to 25 minutes, until the potatoes are tender. Season with the thyme, salt and pepper.

3 Stir in the milk and let simmer for 5 minutes. Stir in the cornstarch mixture and cook, stirring, until thickened. Do not boil.

4 Add the oysters, red pepper and parsley and heat through. Serve piping hot.

Note

Garnish with plain or garlic croutons. A dash of paprika will add color and spice to this dish. This soup can also be served as a main course.

Hearty soups

Red Wine Soup

4 SERVINGS

2 tbsp	butter
1	leek, thinly sliced
1	celery stalk, thinly sliced
2	carrots, peeled and cubed
1	white turnip, peeled and cubed
	salt and freshly ground pepper, to taste
1½ cups	dry red wine
2 cups	beef broth
3 tbsp	pearl barley
	fresh thyme (garnish)

1 In a large heavy saucepan, melt the butter over medium-low heat. Add the vegetables, and cook, stirring often for 5 to 10 minutes, until slightly softened. Season with salt and pepper.

2 Add the beef broth and red wine. Increase the heat and bring to a boil.

3 Add the barley, lower the heat, cover and simmer for 20 to 25 minutes, until the vegetables and barley are tender.

4 Taste for seasoning. Garnish with fresh thyme. Serve with bread and a selection of cheeses.

Note

The simple addition of cubes of cooked meat at the end of cooking makes this soup a full meal.

Corn and Vegetable Soup

4 SERVINGS

4 tbsp	butter
1	onion, chopped
2	garlic cloves, chopped
2	celery stalks, thinly sliced
2	carrots, peeled and cubed
½	rutabaga, peeled and cubed
1	zucchini, cubed
⅔ cup	sliced cabbage
1 cup	frozen or drained canned corn niblets
	salt and freshly ground pepper, to taste
1	bay leaf
1 tsp	dried oregano
4 cups	vegetable broth

1 In a large heavy saucepan, melt the butter over medium heat. Add the onion and the garlic and cook, stirring often, until tender.

2 Stir in the remaining vegetables and cook, stirring often, for 5 to 10 minutes, until slightly softened. Season with salt and pepper and add the herbs.

3 Stir in the vegetable broth and bring to a boil. Lower the heat and simmer for 10 minutes, until the vegetables are tender.

4 Taste for seasoning, and remove the bay leaf. Serve piping hot.

Note
For a heartier soup, sprinkle some grated cheese on top.

Beer Soup

4 SERVINGS

2 tbsp	vegetable oil
1	onion, chopped
2	garlic cloves, chopped
½ lb	skinned and boned chicken breast halves, cubed
½ cup	cooked ham, cubed
1	celery stalk, thinly sliced
1	carrot, peeled and cubed
1	potato, peeled and cubed
	salt and freshly ground pepper, to taste
1	bay leaf
1 tsp	dried thyme
2 cups	chicken broth
1 bottle	pale ale
¼ cup	heavy cream
2 tbsp	chopped fresh parsley

1 Heat the oil in a large heavy saucepan over high heat. Add the onion and garlic and cook and stir until golden. Add the chicken and ham cubes and sauté until the chicken is golden.

2 Add the remaining vegetables, lower the heat and cook, stirring often, for 5 to 10 minutes, until the vegetables are slightly softened. Season with salt and pepper and add the herbs.

3 Add the chicken broth and the beer and bring to a boil. Lower the heat and let simmer for about 10 minutes, until the vegetables are tender and the chicken is thoroughly cooked.

4 Remove the bay leaf, and taste for seasoning. Add the cream and the parsley just before serving.

Hearty soups

Spiced Soup

4 SERVINGS

1 tbsp	vegetable oil
1	onion, finely chopped
1	garlic clove, minced
½ tsp	ground cumin
1½ tsp	curry powder
¼ tsp	grated fresh ginger,
2½ cups	chicken broth
1 cup	tomato juice or vegetable juice
1	potato, peeled and cut in julienne strips
1	carrot, cut in julienne strips
¼ cup	frozen or drained canned corn niblets
	salt and freshly ground pepper, to taste
	cilantro leaves for garnish

1 In a large heavy saucepan, over medium-low heat, stir the oil, onion, garlic, curry powder, cumin and ginger. Cook, stirring, until the onion is soft.

2 Add the chicken broth and the tomato or vegetable juice. Increase the heat and bring to a boil.

3 Add the potato and the carrot. Lower the heat, cover and simmer for 10 to 15 minutes, until the vegetables are tender.

4 Add the corn, cover and continue cooking for another few minutes, until heated through. Season to taste with salt and pepper. Ladle into bowls and serve garnished with cilantro leaves.

Hearty soups

Hearty Seafood Potage

2 SERVINGS

2 tbsp	olive oil
1	onion, finely chopped
1 can (14 oz)	artichoke hearts, drained
1 cup	chicken broth
¼ cup	dry white wine
¾ cup	light cream
2 tbsp	chopped fresh parsley
½ tsp	ground nutmeg
	salt and freshly ground pepper, to taste
½ lb	seafood, such as: raw peeled small or halved shrimp, diced sea scallops, flaked cooked crabmeat and/or chopped cooked lobster meat
	chopped fresh parsley springs (garnish)

1 Heat the oil in a large heavy saucepan over low heat. Add the onion and cook for approximately 5 minutes, until tender. Add the artichokes, the chicken broth and white wine. Increase the heat and bring to a boil.

2 Lower the heat, cover and let simmer for 5 minutes. Purée the soup in batches in a food processor. Return to the saucepan.

3 Add the cream, chopped parsley and nutmeg, and season to taste with salt and pepper. Let simmer on low heat for 8 minutes.

4 Add the seafood and simmer slowly for 3 to 5 minutes without boiling, until cooked through (or warmed). Garnish with parsley sprigs and serve.

Note
Do not boil this soup, as the texture of the seafood will become rubbery.

Hearty soups

Autumn Soup

4 SERVINGS

4 tbsp	butter
2	onions, thinly sliced
2	garlic cloves, chopped
3 cups	chicken broth
1 cup	peeled and cubed potatoes
2 cups	peeled and cubed butternut squash
	pinch of ground nutmeg
	salt and freshly ground pepper, to taste
1 cup	milk or half-and-half
	fresh chopped chives (garnish)

1 In a large heavy saucepan melt the butter over low heat. Add the onions and garlic and cook, stirring often, for 5 minutes or until tender but not browned.

2 Add the chicken broth and the squash and potatoes. Increase the heat and bring to a boil. Lower the heat, cover and simmer for 20 to 30 minutes, until the vegetables are tender. Season with the nutmeg, salt and pepper.

3 Purée the soup in batches in a food processor. Return to the saucepan and bring to a boil over medium heat.

4 Add the milk or half-and-half, stirring constantly, and heat through without boiling. Taste for seasoning. When serving, garnish each bowl with a pinch of chopped chives.

Note

This same recipe can be used with different varieties of squash. Pumpkin, delicata or acorn squash would all be good.

Cream Soups

Garlic Soup

4 SERVINGS

2 tbsp	butter
1	head of garlic, peeled and finely chopped
4 cups	chicken broth
¼ cup	dry white wine
1	bay leaf
1 tsp	dried thyme
2 cups	crumbled dry bread crusts
	salt and freshly ground pepper, to taste
2	egg yolks
¼ cup	heavy cream
4	sprigs of parsley and chopped parsley (garnish)

1 In a large heavy saucepan, melt the butter over low heat. Add the garlic and cook, stirring often, for 5 minutes, until tender but not browned.

2 Stir in the chicken broth and white wine. Increase the heat and bring to a boil. Add the herbs and season to taste with salt and pepper.

3 Add the bread and simmer over medium heat, stirring often, and mashing the garlic with a spoon, for approximately 15 minutes, until the bread and garlic are soft. Whisk the egg yolks and cream in a small bowl.

4 Whisk the egg yolks with a little hot soup to warm them. Transfer to the soup, stirring constantly, until thickened and glossy. Remove from the heat. Taste for seasoning. Serve immediately, garnished with parsley.

Cream Soups

Thai Pumpkin Soup

4 to 6 SERVINGS

4 tbsp	butter
2 cups	peeled and cubed acorn squash or pumpkin
1	chile pepper, whole
2 cups	canned unsweetened coconut milk
1 cup	chicken broth
	salt and freshly ground pepper, to taste
	thinly sliced zest and juice of 1 lime
1 cup	cooked peeled small shrimp
1	bunch of green onions, thinly sliced

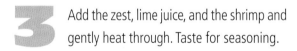

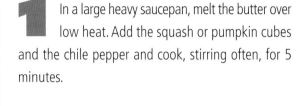
In a large heavy saucepan, melt the butter over low heat. Add the squash or pumpkin cubes and the chile pepper and cook, stirring often, for 5 minutes.

Add the coconut milk and chicken broth, increase the heat and bring to a boil. Lower the heat, cover and simmer gently for 10 to 15 minutes, or until the squash is tender. Season with salt and pepper. Remove the chile.

Add the zest, lime juice, and the shrimp and gently heat through. Taste for seasoning.

When serving, garnish each bowl with some of the sliced green onions.

Cream Soups

Orchard Soup

4 SERVINGS

4 tbsp	butter
2	leeks, thinly sliced
2	celery stalks, thinly sliced
2	carrots, peeled and cubed
1	potato, peeled and cubed
	salt and freshly ground pepper, to taste
4 cups	chicken broth
4	apples, peeled, cored and cubed
	fresh savory or thyme leaves (garnish)

1 In a large heavy saucepan, melt the butter over medium heat. Stir in the leeks and cook, stirring often, for 8 minutes, until tender.

2 Stir in the remaining vegetables. Cover and cook, stirring often, for 5 minutes. Season with salt and pepper.

3 Add the chicken broth, increase the heat and bring to a boil. Lower the heat and simmer for 5 to 10 minutes, until the vegetables are tender.

4 Add the apples and simmer 4 or 5 minutes longer. Taste for seasoning. Ladle into bowls and garnish with savory or thyme.

Note
Make this soup a full meal by adding cubes of cooked chicken and cooked rice.

Cream Soups

Cream of Tomato and Basil Express

4 SERVINGS

4 tbsp	butter
1	onion, finely chopped
2 tbsp	all-purpose flour
1 can (28 oz)	crushed tomatoes
1 cup	milk or light cream
	salt and freshly ground pepper, to taste
¼ cup	chopped fresh basil

1 In a large heavy saucepan, melt the butter over low heat. Stir in the onion and cook, stirring often, until tender.

2 Sprinkle the onion with the flour and cook for 1 minute, stirring constantly. Add the tomatoes. Increase the heat to medium and bring to a boil, stirring constantly.

3 Lower the heat. Stir in the milk and simmer gently for approximately 10 minutes, until lightly thickened. Season with salt and pepper.

4 Stir in the basil just before serving.

Note
This cream of tomatoes does not take long to prepare, as it is not necessary to purée it in a food processor.

Cream Soups

Cream of Celery

4 SERVINGS

1 tbsp	butter
1 cup	sliced celery
1	sliced onion
1	potato, peeled and thinly sliced
2 cups	chicken broth
1½ cups	milk
	salt and freshly ground pepper, to taste
¼ cup	sour cream
1 tbsp	chopped fresh parsley

1 In a large heavy saucepan, melt the butter over medium heat. Add the celery and the onion, and cook, stirring often, for 5 to 7 minutes, until tender.

2 Add the potato and the chicken broth and bring to a boil. Lower the heat, cover and let simmer for 15 to 20 minutes, until the potato is tender. Add the milk, season with salt and pepper and heat through. Do not boil.

3 Purée the soup in batches in a food processor. Return to the saucepan.

4 Reheat if necessary. Ladle into soup bowls and garnish each dish with a spoonful of sour cream and parsley and serve.

Cream Soups

Cream of Avocado

4 SERVINGS

1 tbsp	butter
1	onion, sliced
2	garlic cloves, chopped
2	ripe avocados, halved, pitted, peeled and thinly sliced
2 tbsp	lemon juice
2 tbsp	dry sherry
2 cups	chicken broth
	salt and freshly ground pepper, to taste
1 tbsp	cornstarch
2 cups	milk
¼ cup	heavy cream

1 In a large heavy saucepan, melt the butter over medium heat. Stir in the onion and garlic and cook, stirring often, until lightly browned. Stir in the avocados. Add the lemon juice, sherry and chicken broth. Season with salt and pepper and cook for 5 minutes (do not boil).

2 Purée the soup in batches in a food processor. Return to the saucepan.

3 Mix the cornstarch with the milk and stir into the soup. Bring the soup almost to a boil, over medium heat, stirring constantly, until thickened. Remove from the heat.

4 Ladle into soup bowls and drizzle with 1 tbsp of cream and a grinding of fresh pepper over each. Serve immediately.

Note
Avocado does not tolerate heat well; do not boil it, as it will turn bitter.

Spinach Soup

4 SERVINGS

1 tbsp	vegetable oil
1 tsp	whole cumin seeds
1	garlic clove, finely chopped
6 cups	finely shredded spinach
2½ cups	chicken broth
½ cup	sour cream
½ cup	plain yogurt
	salt and freshly ground pepper, to taste

1 In a large heavy saucepan, heat the oil over medium heat and sauté the cumin seeds until they are fragrant and slightly golden.

2 Add the garlic and cook, stirring, for 1 to 2 minutes. Stir in the spinach in batches. Lower the heat and cook, stirring often, for 5 minutes, until wilted.

3 Add the chicken broth and bring to a boil. Lower the heat, cover and simmer for 10 minutes, until the flavors have blended. Remove from the heat.

4 Add the sour cream and the yogurt a little at a time, stirring briskly. Season with salt and peppers. Serve hot or cold.

Note
For a lighter soup, omit the sour cream and use 1 cup of plain yogurt.

Cream of Beet

2 SERVINGS

1	large beet, boiled until nearly tender, peeled, cut in pieces
1 tbsp	butter
½	onion, finely chopped
2 cups	chicken broth
2 tbsp	long- or short-grain rice
1 tbsp	red wine vinegar
	salt and freshly ground pepper, to taste
½ tsp	Dijon mustard
1	egg yolk
3 tbsp	light cream
2 tbsp	fresh parsley, chopped
	croutons (garnish)

1 Melt the butter in a heavy medium saucepan over low heat. Add the onion and cook and stir for 3 minutes. Pour in the chicken broth, add the rice, increase the heat and bring to a boil.

2 Add the beet and the vinegar and season with salt and pepper. Lower the heat, cover and let simmer for 20 minutes.

3 Purée the soup in batches in a food processor. Strain into the saucepan. Taste for seasoning and whisk in the mustard. Return to the heat and bring to a boil.

4 In a small bowl, whisk the egg yolk and cream with a little hot soup to warm then transfer to the soup, using a whisk or fork, and add to the saucepan, whisking constantly. Remove from the heat. Ladle into bowls. Garnish with parsley and croutons. Serve immediately.

Cream Soups

Potage Parmentier
with Green Onion

4 SERVINGS

4 tbsp	butter
2	bunches green onions, sliced thinly
4 cups	chicken broth
2 cups	peeled and cubed potatoes
	salt and freshly ground pepper, to taste
¼ cup	dry white wine (optional)
1 cup	half-and-half
	chopped fresh chives (garnish)

1 In a large heavy saucepan melt the butter over low heat. Add the green onions and cook, stirring often, for 15 minutes or until they are tender but not browned.

2 Add the chicken broth and the potatoes. Increase the heat and bring to a boil. Lower the heat, cover and simmer for 20 to 30 minutes, until the potatoes are tender.

3 Purée the soup in batches in food processor. Return to the saucepan, add the wine, if desired, and bring to a boil over medium heat. Season to taste with salt and pepper.

4 Add the half-and-half and heat through without boiling. Taste for seasoning. When serving, garnish each bowl with chopped chives.

Note
If you want to turn this soup into a complete meal, just add chunks of cooked meat: chicken, ham, beef. Accompany with crusty bread and a small green salad.

Cream Soups

Leek Velouté

6 SERVINGS

1 tbsp	vegetable oil
4	white parts of leeks, thinly sliced
2	onions, quartered
2	large potatoes, peeled and cubed
6 cups	vegetable broth
1 cup	milk
	salt and freshly ground pepper, to taste
¼ cup	grated gruyère or Swiss cheese,
½	leek, cut in fine strips and blanched (garnish)

1 In a large heavy saucepan, heat the oil over medium heat. Add the leeks and onions and cook, stirring often for 10 minutes, until slightly softened.

2 Add the potatoes and the vegetable broth. Increase the heat and bring to a boil. Lower the heat, cover and simmer for 15 to 20 minutes, until the vegetables are tender.

3 Purée the soup in batches in a food processor. Return to the saucepan. Whisk in the milk. Season to taste with salt and pepper and heat through over low heat.

4 When serving, garnish each bowl with grated cheese and the fine leek strips.

Note

To clean the leeks, cut off the roots and cut in half, dividing white and green parts. Halve the white part lengthwise, and run them under cold water to remove any sand. Save the greens for soup stock.

Cream of Mussels with Saffron

4 SERVINGS

1 tbsp	butter
2	shallots, chopped or 1 small red onion, chopped
2-2½ lb	mussels in the shell, scrubbed with a stiff brush, debearded
1 cup	dry white wine
1 cup	fish stock or clam broth
	pinch of saffron
1½ cups	light cream
	salt and freshly ground pepper, to taste
2 tbsp	slivered fresh parsley (garnish)

1 In a Dutch oven, melt the butter over medium heat. Add the shallots and cook and stir until tender. Add the mussels and the wine, cover and cook for 5 minutes, stirring often, until the mussels have opened.

2 Remove the mussels from the pot, and discard any that are still closed. Then remove the mussels from their shells; cover to keep warm.

3 Add the fish stock and the saffron to the liquid in the pot. Bring to a boil over medium heat. Simmer briskly for 5 minutes.

4 Stir in the cream, lower the heat and simmer slowly for another 5 minutes (without boiling). Return the mussels to the pot, and heat through. Season to taste with salt and pepper and serve hot, garnished with the parsley.

Cream Soups

Cream of Mushroom

4 SERVINGS

2 tbsp	butter
1	small onion, sliced thinly
½ cup	thinly sliced leek
½ cup	sliced celery
1½ cups	thinly sliced mushrooms
3 cups	chicken broth
½ cup	thinly sliced peeled potato
½ cup	light cream
	salt and freshly ground pepper, to taste
2 tbsp	slivered fresh parsley (garnish)

1 In a large heavy saucepan, melt the butter over high heat. Sauté the mushrooms, onion, leek and celery until the vegetables are wilted.

2 Add the chicken broth and the potatoes and let simmer over medium heat for 15 minutes, until the vegetables are tender.

3 Purée the soup in batches in a food processor. Return to the saucepan.

4 Add the cream and heat through. Season to taste with salt and pepper. Ladle into bowls, sprinkle with the parsley and serve.

Note
For a lighter soup, add ½ cup yogurt instead of the cream but don't heat the soup after it's been added.

Cream Soups

Yellow Split Pea and Onion Cream

4 SERVINGS

⅓ cup	yellow split peas, sorted and rinsed
2 cups	water
1 cup	chopped onions
⅓ cup	chopped carrots
2 tsp	butter
1 cup	vegetable broth
1	bay leaf
½ tsp	dill weed
¼ tsp	dried thyme
	salt and freshly ground pepper, to taste
⅓ cup	milk
¼ cup	sour cream
1	small carrot, grated (garnish)

1 Place the split peas and the water in a heavy medium saucepan. Bring to a boil over high heat. Reduce the heat and cover, let simmer for 30 minutes. Do not drain.

2 In a medium non-stick skillet, melt the butter over medium heat. Add the onion and the carrots and cook, stirring often, for 10 minutes, or until the onion is nicely browned. Add to the peas.

3 Add the broth and the herbs. Bring to a boil over high heat. Lower the heat, partially cover and let simmer for 30 minutes, until the split peas are very tender.

4 Season with salt and pepper and remove the bay leaf. Purée the soup in batches in a food processor. Return to the saucepan and stir in the milk. Warm through over medium heat. Garnish with sour cream and the grated carrot.

Cream Soups

Cream of Endive

6 SERVINGS

6	Belgian endives
1 tbsp	butter
3	medium potatoes, peeled and chopped
2	white turnips, peeled and chopped
2	white parts of leeks, chopped
2	onions, peeled and cut in eighths
6 cups	chicken broth
	salt and freshly ground pepper, to taste
2 tbsp	chopped fresh parsley

1 Wipe the endives clean. Cut out the small cone at the base of the endives to remove their bitter taste. Cook the endives for 25 minutes in boiling salted water, with 2 tbsp of lemon juice until tender. Drain and cut into small pieces.

2 Melt the butter in a large heavy saucepan over medium heat. Add the endives, sauté for 3 to 5 minutes, until well coated with butter. Remove and set the endives aside.

3 In the same saucepan, combine the remaining vegetables and the chicken broth. Bring to a boil over high heat. Lower the heat, cover and let simmer for 20 to 25 minutes, until the vegetables are tender.

4 Remove the vegetables (reserving the cooking liquid in the saucepan) and purée in a food processor with the endives. Return the purée to the saucepan, mix well and season with salt and pepper. Sprinkle with parsley and serve.

Note

Endives have a tendency to discolor during cooking if you do not add a bit of lemon juice. They can be kept for 5 to 7 days in the refrigerator.

Cream Soups

Flemish Soup

6 SERVINGS

2 tbsp	butter
1 lb	Brussels sprouts, trimmed
1	onion, peeled and sliced
2	potatoes, peeled and coarsely chopped
5 cups	chicken broth
1	bay leaf
2	whole cloves
	salt and freshly ground pepper, to taste
¼ cup	plain yogurt (garnish)

1 Melt the butter in a large heavy saucepan over high heat. Add the Brussels sprouts and cook, stirring, for 5 minutes.

2 Add the potatoes and onion and and cook and stir for 5 more minutes; add the broth, bay leaf and cloves. Bring to a boil. Lower the heat. Cover and simmer for 45 minutes, until the vegetables are tender.

3 Purée the soup in batches in a food processor. Return to the saucepan.

4 Season to taste with salt and pepper and warm over medium heat. Serve piping hot, garnished with a dollop of yogurt.

Cream Soups

Cream of Watercress

4 SERVINGS

2 tbsp	butter
½ cup	chopped onion
½ cup	grated peeled potatoes
1 tbsp	chopped fresh parsley
2 cups	chopped watercress
2 cups	chicken broth
1 tsp	dried oregano
	salt and freshly ground pepper, to taste
1 cup	half-and-half

1 In a large heavy saucepan, melt the butter over low heat. Add the onion, potato and the parsley. Cover and let cook, stirring occasionally, for 5 minutes.

2 Add the watercress, chicken broth and the oregano. Increase the heat and bring to a boil. Reduce the heat, cover and let simmer, for 20 minutes.

3 Purée the soup in batches in a food processor. Return to the saucepan and reheat slowly. Season to taste with salt and pepper.

4 Stir in the half-and-half and heat through, without letting the soup boil. Serve piping hot.

Note

This is a good basic recipe for a variety of creamed soups. You can replace the watercress with lettuce, spinach, leek, or any other leafy vegetable.

Cream Soups

Rutabaga Velouté

4 SERVINGS

1 tbsp	vegetable oil
1	garlic clove, chopped
1	onion, chopped
2	potatoes, peeled and cubed
1	medium rutabaga, peeled and cubed
2	celery stalks, cubed
2 tbsp	chopped fresh parsley
3 cups	chicken broth
	salt and freshly ground pepper, to taste

1 In a large heavy saucepan, heat the oil over medium heat. Add the garlic and onion and cook, stirring often, until tender.

2 Stir in the potatoes, rutabaga, celery and parsley, and the broth. Bring to a boil.

3 Lower the heat, cover and simmer for 20 to 30 minutes, until the vegetables are very tender.

4 Purée the soup in batches in a food processor. Return to the saucepan. Season to taste with salt and pepper and warm over medium heat until piping hot. Serve.

Note
The addition of a swirl of heavy cream will give your soup a lovely texture.

Cream Soups

Velouté Milanaise

8 SERVINGS

4 cups	chicken broth
1 tbsp	butter
2	skinned and boned chicken breast halves
½ cup	julienne-cut ham
1½ cups	sliced mushroom,
3 tbsp	cornstarch
1 cup	light cream
½ cup	tomato purée
	salt and freshly ground pepper, to taste
¼ cup	grated parmesan cheese

1 In a large heavy saucepan, bring the chicken broth to a boil. Cover and keep warm.

2 Melt the butter in a large nonstick skillet over medium heat. Cook the chicken, turning once, for 8 minutes, until cooked through. Remove and set aside. Add the mushrooms and ham to the skillet, sauté for 5 minutes.

3 Whisk the cornstarch into the cream. Return broth to medium heat. Whisk in cornstarch mixture and tomato purée. Cook, stirring, until thickened and bubbly.

4 Cut the chicken into fine julienne. Add the chicken, ham and mushrooms to the broth Season to taste with salt and pepper and heat through. Ladle into bowls and sprinkle with parmesan.

Cream Soups

Cream of Barley

4 SERVINGS

1 cup	pearl barley
4 cups	chicken broth
2	celery stalks, thinly sliced
½ cup	milk
½ cup	light cream
	celery salt, to taste
	freshly ground pepper, to taste
	finely slivered sage leaves or parsley (garnish)

1 In a medium bowl, cover the barley with water and let soak for 1 hour. Drain.

2 Put the chicken broth, celery and drained barley in a large heavy saucepan. Bring to a boil over high heat. Lower the heat, cover and simmer for 1 hour, until the barley is very tender.

3 Purée the soup in batches in a food processor. Return to the saucepan.

4 Add the milk and cream and season with celery salt and pepper. Reheat slowly and serve. Garnish with slivered sage or parsley.

Cream Soups

Cream of Tomato
Florentine

4 SERVINGS

2 tsp	vegetable oil
¼ cup	chopped onions
½ cup	chopped celery
1	garlic clove, minced
1 can (28 oz)	crushed tomatoes
1½ cups	chicken broth
¼ cup	minute rice
½ tsp	dried oregano
½ tsp	dried basil
	salt and freshly ground pepper, to taste
1 tbsp	cornstarch mixed with 2 tbsp water
4	French baguette slices, lightly toasted
¼ cup	shredded mozzarella cheese
2½ cups	loosely packed shredded spinach, lightly cooked
¼ cup	sour cream

1 In a large heavy saucepan, heat the oil over medium heat. Add the celery and onion, sauté until golden. Add the garlic, tomatoes, broth, rice and herbs. Bring to a boil. Lower the heat, cover and simmer 20 minutes.

2 Purée the soup in batches in a food processor. Return to the saucepan. Place over medium heat. Stir in the cornstarch mixture and season with salt and pepper. Cook, stirring, until thickened and bubbly.

3 Turn the oven to broil. Sprinkle the bread slices with the mozzarella, arrange on a baking sheet and broil lightly.

4 Just before serving, add the spinach and the sour cream to the soup. Serve in soup bowls and garnish with the mozzarella toasts.

Cream Soups

Mint-flavored Mushroom
and Escargot Velouté

4 to 6 SERVINGS

1 tbsp   butter

2 cups   coarsely sliced mushrooms

½ cup   sliced celery

2   green onions, thinly sliced

5 cups   chicken broth

1 cup   cubed peeled potatoes

1 cup   loosely packed fresh parsley sprigs

¼ cup   thinly sliced fresh mint

    salt and freshly ground pepper, to taste

½ cup   light cream

24   drained canned escargots

1 In a large heavy saucepan, melt the butter over medium heat. Add the mushrooms, celery and green onions and cook, stirring often, until wilted.

2 Add the chicken broth and the potatoes, parsley and mint. Season with salt and pepper. Bring to a boil. Lower the heat and let simmer for approximately 25 minutes, or until the potatoes are tender.

3 Purée the soup in batches in a food processor. Return to the saucepan.

4 Just before serving, add the cream and the escargots, and heat through, without boiling.

Cream Soups

Cream of Fennel
and Snow Crab

4 to 6 SERVINGS

1 tbsp	butter
½ cup	coarsely chopped onion
½ cup	sliced celery
½ cup	sliced leek
1	fennel bulb, trimmed and sliced (feathery fronds chopped and reserved for garnish)
1 cup	diced peeled potatoes
½ cup	fresh parsley sprigs
5 cups	chicken broth
½ cup	light cream
	salt and freshly ground pepper, to taste
½ cup	chopped cooked snow crab

1 In a large heavy saucepan, melt the butter over medium heat. Add the fennel, onion, celery and leek and cook, stirring often, until wilted.

2 Add the potato, parsley and chicken broth. Bring to a boil. Lower the heat and simmer 25 minutes, until the vegetables are tender.

3 Purée the soup in batches in a food processor. Return to the saucepan.

4 Stir in the cream, season to taste with salt and pepper and warm through over medium heat. Stir in the crab. Serve hot, decorated with fennel fronds, if desired.

Cream Soups

Cream of Squash and Pepper
with Maple Syrup

4 to 6 SERVINGS

2 tbsp	olive oil
2	zucchini, cut into large cubes
2	red, green or yellow peppers, coarsely chopped
½ cup	coarsely chopped celery
2	green onions, coarsely chopped
2 tbsp	coarsely chopped fresh parsley
1 cup	peeled and cubed potato
½ tsp	minced garlic
6 cups	chicken broth
¼ cup	maple syrup-based liqueur or white wine
2 tbsp	pure maple syrup
1 tsp	white vinegar
	salt and freshly ground pepper, to taste
½ cup	light cream
1	small bunch of basil or parsley (garnish)

1 In a large heavy saucepan, heat the oil over medium heat. Add the zucchini, peppers, celery and green onions and cook, stirring often, until slightly softened.

2 Add the parsley, potatoes, garlic, chicken broth; liqueur, maple syrup, vinegar and season with salt and pepper. Bring to a boil. Lower the heat, cover, and let simmer for 25 minute, until the vegetables are tender.

3 Purée the soup in batches in a food processor. Return to the saucepan.

4 Add the cream and heat through over low heat just before serving. Decorate with small sprigs of basil or parsley.

Cream Soups

Cream of Fennel and Cucumber

4 to 6 SERVINGS

1 tbsp	butter
1	fennel bulb, trimmed and sliced
¾ cup	chopped onion
¾ cup	sliced celery
2	English cucumbers, coarsely sliced
1 cup	cubed peeled potato
1 tbsp	coarsely chopped fresh parsley
5 cups	chicken broth
1 cup	milk
	salt and freshly ground pepper, to taste

Garnish

1	tomato, seeded and cubed
2 tbsp	chopped fresh cilantro or fresh parsley

1 In a large heavy saucepan, melt the butter over medium heat. Add the fennel, onion and celery and cook, stirring often, until tender. Add the cucumbers, potato and parsley.

2 Add the chicken broth and bring to a boil. Lower the heat, cover and let simmer, for 20 to 25 minutes, until the vegetables are tender.

3 Purée the soup in batches in a food processor. Return to the saucepan.

4 Stir in the milk, season with salt and pepper and warm through over medium heat. Pour into soup bowls and garnish with the cubes of tomato and cilantro.

Note
This soup can be served hot, or chilled as a vichyssoise.

Cream Soups

Lemon Balm and Carrot
Velouté

4 to 6 SERVINGS

1 tbsp	butter
2 cups	coarsely chopped carrots
1	onion, coarsely chopped
1 cup	coarsely chopped celery
4 cups	chicken broth
1 can (28 oz)	whole tomatoes, with juices
1 cup	peeled coarsely cut potato
	salt and freshly ground pepper, to taste
½ cup	light cream
2 tbsp	orange juice
2 tbsp	chopped fresh lemon balm
1 tbsp	grated orange zest
1 tbsp	grated lime zest
4	small sprigs of lemon balm (garnish)

1 In a large heavy saucepan, melt the butter over medium-low heat. Add the carrots, onion and celery and cook, stirring often, until softened.

2 Add the chicken broth, the tomatoes and the potato. Increase the heat and bring to a boil. Lower the heat, cover and let simmer for 20 minutes; until the potato is tender.

3 Remove the vegetables (reserve the liquid in the saucepan) and purée them in a food processor. Return the purée to the saucepan and mix well; heat over low heat. Season with salt and pepper.

4 Stir in the cream, orange juice and lemon balm. Just before serving, sprinkle with the orange and lime zests. Garnish with the lemon balm sprigs.

Note
If you can't find lemon balm, substitute fresh mint.

Cream Soups

Asparagus Velouté

4 SERVINGS

2 tbsp	butter
1	small red onion, chopped
2	celery stalks, thinly sliced
1	green onion, chopped
1	garlic clove, chopped
1 tbsp	all-purpose flour
3 cups	milk
2 cups	thinly sliced cooked asparagus, (reserve the tips for the garnish)
1 tbsp	dry sherry
1	bay leaf
½ tsp	dried thyme
1 tsp	fresh lemon juice
	salt and freshly ground pepper, to taste

1 In a large heavy saucepan, melt the butter over medium heat. Add the red onion, celery, green onion and garlic and cook, stirring often, for 2 to 3 minutes.

2 Add the flour, mix well and cook, stirring, 1 minute. Gradually add the milk, stirring constantly. Add the asparagus, sherry and herbs; bring to a boil. Lower the heat, cover and let simmer for 20 minutes.

3 Remove the bay leaf and purée the soup in batches in a food processor. Return to the saucepan.

4 Stir in the lemon juice and season with salt and pepper. Ladle into soup bowls and garnish with the asparagus tips. Serve immediately.

Cream Soups

Potage Grenoblois

4 SERVINGS

3 tbsp	butter
1	onion, sliced
2	celery stalks, sliced
2 cups	chicken broth
1 cup	milk
¼ cup	chopped walnuts
2 tbsp	cornstarch mixed with 3 tbsp cold water
2	egg yolks
¾ cup	heavy cream
	salt and freshly ground pepper, to taste
	chopped walnuts (garnish)

1 In a large heavy saucepan, melt the butter over medium-high heat. Add the onion and cook, stirring often for 5 minutes, until lightly golden. Add the celery and cook for 2 minutes longer.

2 Stir in the broth, milk, walnuts and cornstarch mixture into the saucepan. Bring to a boil, stirring. Lower the heat, cover and simmer for 15 minutes.

3 Purée the soup in batches in a food processor. Return to the saucepan.

4 Stir in the eggs and cream. Season to taste with salt and pepper and warm through over medium heat, stirring often. Serve in bowls and garnish with the chopped walnuts.

Note
For a milder tasting soup, replace the walnuts with almonds or hazelnuts.

Cream Soups

Cream of Spinach
with Peaches

4 to 6 SERVINGS

2 tbsp	butter
½ cup	coarsely chopped onion
½ cup	coarsely chopped celery
½ cup	coarsely chopped leek
6 cups	chicken broth
1 cup	coarsely chopped peeled potato
1 bag (5–6 oz)	baby spinach
	salt and freshly ground pepper, to taste
1 cup	light cream (optional)
2	fresh or canned peaches

1 Melt the butter in a large heavy saucepan over low heat. Add the onion, celery and leek, and sauté gently.

2 Add the chicken broth and the potato, increase the heat and bring to a boil. Lower the heat and let simmer for 15 minutes. Add the spinach, and continue cooking for 5 minutes, until the vegetables are tender.

3 Remove the vegetables (reserving the cooking liquid in the saucepan) and purée in a food processor. Return the purée to the saucepan. Add the cream and season with salt and pepper. Heat through over low heat.

4 Peel the peaches, if using fresh, and cut them into thin sections. Pour the cream of spinach into bowls and garnish with the peach sections.

Cream Soups

Cream of Mixed Greens

4 to 6 SERVINGS

1 tbsp	butter
3 cups	coarsely shredded lettuce
½ cup	cubed celery
¼ cup	sliced onion
6 cups	chicken broth
1½ cups	cubed peeled potato
1	sprig of parsley
2 cups	coarsely chopped watercress
1 cup	light cream
	salt and freshly ground pepper, to taste
1 cup	small leek, cut into fine julienne and blanched

1 In a large heavy saucepan, melt the butter over medium-low heat. Add the lettuce, celery and onion and cook, stirring often, until wilted.

2 Add the chicken broth, potatoes and parsley. Increase the heat and bring to a boil. Lower the heat and let simmer 20 minutes. Add the watercress. Continue cooking for another 5 minutes.

3 Purée the soup in batches in a food processor. Return to the saucepan. Heat slowly and add the cream. Season to taste with salt and pepper.

4 Pour the soup into soup bowls and garnish each bowl with a bit of the blanched leek. Serve immediately.

Cream Soups

Potage Crécy à l'Orange

4 SERVINGS

1 tbsp	vegetable oil
8	carrots, peeled and sliced
2	onions, finely sliced
	grated zest of 1 orange
4 cups	vegetable broth
2 tbsp	butter
2 tbsp	all-purpose flour
1 cup	orange juice
	salt and freshly ground pepper, to taste
1	orange, peeled and sliced (garnish)
	thyme sprigs (garnish)

1 Heat the oil in a large heavy saucepan over medium heat. Add the carrots, onions and orange zest and cook until softened. Add the vegetable broth, bring to a simmer. Cover and cook for 20 minutes, until the carrots are very tender.

2 Melt the butter in a small saucepan over medium heat. Add the flour and cook, stirring, for 1 minute. Add the orange juice and cook, stirring until thickened.

3 Purée the carrot mixture in batches in a food processor. Return to the saucepan and stir in the orange juice. Season to taste with salt and pepper. Warm through until piping hot.

4 Ladle into soup bowls and garnish each with an orange slice.

Cream Soups

Watercress and Chervil Velouté

8 to 10 SERVINGS

2 tbsp	butter
1 cup	coarsely chopped onion,
1 cup	sliced celery
1 cup	thinly sliced leek
3 cups	watercress sprigs
2 cups	peeled and cubed potato
8 cups	chicken broth
1 cup	coarsely chopped fresh chervil
	or
1 tbsp	dried chervil
	salt and freshly ground pepper, to taste

Garnish

½ cup	sour cream
8 to 10	sprigs of fresh chervil or parsley

1 In a large heavy saucepan, melt the butter over medium heat. Add the onion, celery and leek and cook, stirring often, until tender. Add the watercress and the potatoes.

2 Add the chicken broth and the chervil; season with salt and pepper and bring to a boil. Lower the heat, cover and simmer for 20 minutes, until the vegetables are tender.

3 Purée the soup in batches in a food processor. Return to the saucepan. Heat over low heat.

4 Serve in bowls and garnish with a splash of sour cream and a sprig of chervil.

Note
Surprise your guests by adding thin strips of smoked salmon. A guaranteed success!

Cream Soups

Cream of Poultry and Lettuce

4 SERVINGS

3 tbsp	butter
½	white of leek, thinly sliced
1	medium carrot, thinly sliced
1	celery stalk, thinly sliced
1	small onion, thinly sliced
2 tbsp	all-purpose flour
½ cup	milk
3 cups	chicken broth
1	bay leaf
1	fresh sage leaf or pinch of dried sage
	pinch of dried thyme
	salt and freshly ground pepper, to taste
½	head of iceberg lettuce, broken up
1 cup	cubed cooked chicken or turkey
	pinch of paprika
	shredded lettuce (garnish)

1 In a large heavy saucepan, melt the butter over low heat. Add all the vegetables except the lettuce and cook for 3 to 4 minutes, until slightly softened. Sprinkle with the flour and mix well.

2 Slowly stir in the milk and broth. Add the herbs and season with salt and pepper. Increase the heat and bring to a boil. Lower the heat, and let simmer for 15 minutes to blend the flavors.

3 Add the lettuce leaves. Purée the soup in batches in a food processor. Return to the saucepan.

4 Add the chicken pieces and the paprika. Reheat and serve piping hot. Garnish bowls with shredded lettuce.

Note
This is an ideal recipe to use up any wilted lettuce on hand.

Cream Soups

Country Velouté

4 to 6 SERVINGS

8 cups	water
	frame from 1 roast turkey
1	onion
1	carrot
1	celery stalk
1	bay leaf
1	sprig of thyme
1	sprig of parsley
	salt and freshly ground pepper, to taste
4 tbsp	butter, softened
¼ cup	all-purpose flour
½ cup	light cream

Garnish

½ cup	cooked small broccoli florets
½ cup	cooked and cubed carrots
½ cup	cooked cubed potato
½ cup	cooked cut wax beans
2 tbsp	chopped fresh parsley (garnish)

1 In a large saucepan, bring the water to a boil. Add the turkey frame, onion, carrot, celery and herbs. Season with salt and pepper. Lower the heat to medium and let simmer 30 minutes.

2 Strain the stock into another saucepan. Return to medium heat. Knead the butter and flour into a paste. Stir into the soup and bring to a boil, stirring often, until slightly thickened.

3 Lower the heat and let simmer for 10 more minutes. Strain again if necessary and taste for seasoning.

4 Just before serving, stir in the cream and the vegetables and warm through. Garnish with the parsley.

Note

A little secret to keep your parsley fresh: once you get your parsley home from the market, wrap it up in moist paper towels and place in a reusable plastic bag, and then store in the vegetable compartment of your fridge. This method will keep your parsley fresh for at least 2 weeks.

Cream Soups

Smoked Salmon Velouté à la Vichy

4 SERVINGS

2	large potatoes, peeled and cubed
1	white of leek, thinly sliced
1	onion, sliced
2 cups	chicken broth
1 cup	milk
1 cup	sour cream
¾ cup	coarsely chopped smoked salmon
1 tbsp	fresh lemon juice
	salt and freshly ground pepper, to taste
⅓ cup	thin strips of smoked salmon
2	green onions, sliced

1 In a large saucepan, combine the potatoes, leek and onion; add the chicken broth. Bring to a boil over high heat. Lower the heat, cover and cook for 20 minutes, until the potatoes are tender.

2 Remove from the heat and add the milk; place in a food processor. Add the sour cream, chopped smoked salmon and the lemon juice. Purée until smooth and creamy, and season with salt and pepper.

3 Transfer to a bowl, cover and refrigerate for at least 4 hours, until well-chilled.

4 Just before serving, ladle the velouté into chilled soup bowls, and garnish with the strips of smoked salmon and the green onions.

Note
Before beginning the meal, place the soup bowls in the freezer to properly chill them. For a more refined look, lay a few salmon eggs (salmon caviar) on top of the velouté.

Cream Soups

Red Pepper Velouté

4 SERVINGS

3 tbsp	vegetable oil
1	onion, finely chopped
½ cup	chopped celery
6	red peppers, seeded and chopped
	salt and freshly ground pepper, to taste
4 cups	chicken broth
1 cup	peeled and cubed potato
½ cup	heavy cream
	small basil leaves (garnish)

1 In a large heavy saucepan, heat the oil over medium-high heat. Add the peppers, onion and celery and cook, stirring often, for 10 minutes, until lightly golden. Season with salt and pepper.

2 Add the chicken broth and the potato, bring to a boil. Lower the heat, cover and let simmer for 15 minutes, until the peppers are tender.

3 Purée the soup in batches in a food processor. Return to the saucepan and heat slowly.

4 Stir in the cream, warm through, and taste for seasoning. Serve immediately in soup bowls. Garnish with the basil leaves.

Cream Soups

Cream of Papaya and Coriander

4 SERVINGS

2 tbsp	vegetable oil
1 tbsp	butter
1	onion, sliced
2	fresh papaya, halved, seeded, peeled, and cubed
1	potato, peeled and cubed
3 cups	chicken broth
	salt and freshly ground pepper, to taste
¼ cup	sour cream
¼ cup	chopped fresh cilantro

1 In a heavy medium saucepan, heat the oil and melt the butter over medium heat. Sauté the onion for 5 minutes, or until tender.

2 Stir in the papaya and the potato. Add the chicken broth and bring to a boil. Lower the heat, cover and simmer for 20 to 30 minutes, until the potato is tender.

3 Purée the soup in batches in a food processor. Return to the saucepan, season to taste with salt and pepper and bring to a boil over low heat.

4 Taste for seasoning. Ladle into bowls and garnish each bowl with sour cream and fresh cilantro.

Note
Mango can replace the papaya in another variation of this recipe.

Cream Soups

Irish Soup

8 SERVINGS

2 tbsp	butter
½ lb	beef flank steak, thinly sliced
8 cups	beef broth
¼ cup	green lentils, sorted and rinsed
¼ cup	pearl barley
2 cups	sliced cabbage
2	onions, thinly sliced
2	carrots, thinly sliced
1	white turnip, peeled and cubed
2	celery stalks, sliced
1	bay leaf
2 tbsp	chopped fresh parsley
1 tsp	dried thyme
	salt and freshly ground pepper, to taste

1 Melt the butter in a large heavy saucepan over high heat.

2 Add the steak slices and cook until browned.

3 Add the beef broth and bring to a boil.

4 Add all the other ingredients, lower the heat, cover and let simmer approximately 40 minutes, until the beef, lentils and barley are tender. Taste for seasoning and serve.

Note

Green lentils do not have to be soaked before cooking; they cook rather quickly.

Traditional Soups

Minestrone alla Casalinga

4 to 6 SERVINGS

½ **cup**	dried white or red kidney beans
3 tbsp	olive oil or vegetable oil
2	onions, chopped
2	garlic cloves, crushed in a garlic press
2 to 3	slices of bacon
4	tomatoes, peeled, seeded and cut thin
8 cups	vegetable broth or water
½ **tsp**	chopped fresh marjoram or basil
	pinch of fresh thyme
2	carrots, peeled and cubed
2	potatoes, peeled and cubed
1	small white turnip, peeled and cubed
1 to 2	celery stalks, cut fine
1¼ cups	finely shredded cabbage
½ **cup**	short macaroni or small pasta
1 tbsp	coarsely chopped fresh parsley
	salt and freshly ground pepper, to taste
	grated parmesan, to taste

1 Soak the dried beans in cold water to cover overnight. Drain.

2 In a large heavy saucepan heat the oil over medium-high heat. Add the onions, garlic and bacon. Cook, stirring often, until the onion is tender and the bacon has rendered its fat.

3 Add the tomatoes and the beans. Pour in the broth or water, and add the herbs. Bring to a boil. Lower the heat, cover and let simmer approximately 1 hour, or until the beans are tender.

4 Add the carrots, and cook for another 10 minutes. Add the potatoes, turnip, celery, cabbage and pasta, and cook until the pasta and all the vegetables are tender. Add the parsley, and season with salt and pepper. Sprinkle with grated parmesan and serve.

Traditional Soups

Chinese Noodle Soup

4 to 6 SERVINGS

2 cups	sliced mushrooms
1 tsp	finely minced garlic
1 tbsp	butter
6 cups	chicken broth
2 cups	fresh chow mein noodles or thin fresh pasta
1 tbsp	lemon juice
	few drops hot pepper sauce or chili oil (optional)
½ cup	chopped green onions
1 tbsp	chopped fresh cilantro
1 tsp	finely slivered fresh ginger, peeled

1 In a large heavy saucepan, melt the butter over high heat. Add the mushrooms and garlic and sauté for 2 minutes, until the mushrooms have wilted.

2 Add the chicken broth and bring to a boil.

3 Add the noodles, lemon juice and the pepper sauce or chili oil, if using.

4 Lower the heat, cover and let simmer for 3 minutes, until the noodles are tender. Add the green onions, coriander and ginger and serve piping hot.

Note

Here's an interesting suggestion: why not add some crab, pollock or small shrimp to this exotic dish?

Traditional Soups

Seafood and Clam
Chowder

4 SERVINGS

2 tbsp	butter
1	small carrot, cubed
1	celery stalk, cubed
½	onion, finely chopped
3 tbsp	all-purpose flour
1 tbsp	ground turmeric
1 can (10 oz)	whole clams, with their juice
1 can (6 oz)	tuna, drained and flaked
1 can (7½ oz)	salmon, drained and flaked
¾ cup	drained canned corn niblets
2 cups	fish stock or 1 cup clam broth and 1 cup water
1	bay leaf
	salt and freshly ground pepper, to taste

1 Melt the butter in a large heavy saucepan over medium heat. Add the carrot, celery and onion and cook, stirring often, for approximately 5 minutes, or until the onion is tender.

2 Sprinkle with the flour and turmeric and mix well. Cook, stirring constantly, for 1 minute

3 Add the clams and their juice, the salmon, tuna, corn, fish stock or clam juice and water and the bay leaf. Bring to a boil. Lower the heat and let simmer, stirring occasionally, for 20 minutes.

4 Remove the bay leaf. Season to taste with salt and pepper. Serve piping hot.

Traditional Soups

Five-Season Soup
(Shi jin tàng)

4 SERVINGS

1 cup	ground raw chicken or turkey
2	bread slices (crusts removed), crumbled
1	egg white
2 tbsp	cornstarch
1 tbsp	minced peeled fresh ginger
1 tbsp	finely chopped shallot
1 tbsp	soy sauce
1 tbsp	rice wine vinegar
1 tbsp	vegetable oil
	freshly ground pepper, to taste
6 cups	chicken broth
1½ cups	finely shredded Chinese cabbage
1 cup	thinly sliced Chinese mushrooms or white mushrooms
1	carrot, thinly sliced
1 can (8 oz)	sliced bamboo shoots, drained
1	white of leek, thinly sliced
2	green onions, thinly sliced (garnish)

Note
Just before serving, you can add additional soy sauce and rice wine vinegar to taste.

1 In a bowl, mix the chicken or turkey, bread, egg white, cornstarch, ginger, shallot, soy sauce, rice wine vinegar, oil and pepper together until well blended.

2 Mold this mixture into meatballs (dumplings) measuring ½ inch in diameter.

3 In a large saucepan, bring the chicken broth to a boil over high heat. Add the dumplings, lower the heat and let simmer for 15 minutes, until the dumplings are cooked through.

4 Add the Chinese cabbage, mushrooms, carrot, bamboo shoots and leek. Cover and let simmer for another 15 minutes, until the vegetables are tender. Serve in bowls and garnish with the thinly sliced green onions.

Traditional Soups

Spicy Shrimp Soup

4 SERVINGS

3 cups	chicken broth
1 cup	sliced mushrooms
1 can (10 oz)	sliced bamboo shoots, drained
2 cups	cooked peeled small shrimp
2 tbsp	cornstarch, mixed with 3 tbsp of cold water
2 tbsp	white wine vinegar
½ tsp	crushed red pepper flakes
	salt and freshly ground pepper, to taste
1	egg, beaten
2	green onions, thinly sliced

1 In a large heavy saucepan, bring the chicken broth to a boil over high heat. Add the mushrooms. Lower the heat and let simmer for 5 minutes.

2 Add the bamboo shoots and the shrimp. Stir in the cornstarch mixture and cook, stirring, until slightly thickened.

3 Add the vinegar, crushed red pepper flakes and season with salt and pepper. Add the egg and cook while stirring with a fork in order to create thin threads. Remove from heat.

4 Sprinkle with the green onions and serve immediately.

Note
The soup must not boil once the egg has been added, to avoid having the filaments break up.

Traditional Soups

4-Step Soup Recipes ■ ■ ■ ■ 151

Black Bean Soup

4 SERVINGS

2 cups	dried black beans, sorted and rinsed
10 cups	water
¼ lb	bacon, cut into ½-in. strips
1 tsp	dry mustard
⅓ cup	chopped onion
1	package of chili seasoning mix
	salt and freshly ground pepper, to taste
2 tbsp	lemon juice
2 tbsp	chopped fresh parsley
1	lemon slice, cut into wedges (garnish)

1 In a large heavy saucepan, combine the beans, water and bacon. Bring to a boil over high heat. Lower the heat, cover and let simmer for 2½ hours.

2 Add the onion, the chili seasoning mix and the dry mustard.

3 Season with salt and pepper, cover and let simmer for another 30 minutes, until the beans are very tender.

4 Taste for seasoning. Just before serving, add the lemon juice and the chopped parsley. Ladle into bowls and garnish each with a piece of lemon.

Traditional Soups

Corn Chowder

4 SERVINGS

2 cups	cubed peeled potatoes
2 cups	vegetable broth
2 tbsp	corn oil
1 can **(11 oz)**	corn niblets, drained
½	onion, chopped
2 tbsp	tomato paste
½	red hot chile pepper, seeded and finely chopped
1	garlic clove, finely chopped
¾ cup	milk
	salt and freshly ground pepper, to taste
	corn chips and salsa, for serving

1 In a heavy medium saucepan, combine the potatoes, broth and oil. Bring to a boil over high heat. Lower the heat, cover and let cook for 10 minutes, until the potatoes are tender.

2 Stir in the corn, onion, the tomato paste, hot pepper and garlic. Bring to a boil and remove from the heat.

3 Stir in the milk and season to taste with salt and pepper.

4 Serve accompanied with corn chips and salsa.

Traditional Soups

Won Ton Soup

4 SERVINGS

½ **cup**	coarsely chopped ham
½ **cup**	coarsely chopped cooked chicken
1 tbsp	soy sauce
½ **tsp**	ground ginger
1	garlic clove, minced
	salt and freshly ground pepper, to taste
20	commercially available egg roll wrappers, thawed if frozen
1	egg, beaten

Broth

6 cups	chicken broth
1 tbsp	soy sauce
2 tsp	Asian sesame oil
½ **tsp**	sugar
3	green onions, thinly sliced on the diagonal (garnish)

1 In a food processor, finely chop the ham, chicken, soy sauce, ginger, garlic and pepper.

2 Place 1 tbsp of the ham mixture on each egg roll wrapper. Lightly brush the edges with egg and bring and fold all corners into the center (see photo). Seal the edges tightly. Let sit for 15 minutes.

3 In a large saucepan, bring 4 cups salted water to a boil over high heat. Spoon the won tons into the water and cook for 5 minutes, until they float to the surface. Transfer won tons to a colander, drain. Discard the water.

4 In the same saucepan, combine the chicken broth, soy sauce, sesame oil and sugar. Bring to a boil over high heat. Lower the heat and add the won tons. Reheat the soup gently. Ladle into bowls and garnish with the green onions.

Traditional Soups

Vietnamese Asparagus Soup

4 SERVINGS

4 cups	chicken broth
¼ lb	vermicelli
2 tsp	vegetable oil
2	slices of cooked ham, julienned
2 cups	asparagus tips, cooked crisp-tender
1	onion, chopped
1 tbsp	soy sauce
1	garlic clove, minced
	salt and freshly ground pepper, to taste

1 In a large saucepan, bring the broth to a boil over high heat. Add the vermicelli, lower the heat and cook, stirring often for 3 minutes, until al dente.

2 Heat the oil in a small skillet over high heat, and sauté the julienned ham. Add to the broth.

3 Add all the other ingredients, and let simmer for 5 minutes.

4 Season to taste with salt and pepper. Ladle into bowls and serve.

Traditional Soups

Mexican Soup
(Sopa De Hambre Gringo)

4 SERVINGS

1 cup	dried black beans, picked over and rinsed
6 cups	beef broth
2	carrots, peeled and finely sliced
2	medium onions, chopped
2	garlic cloves, chopped
1 can (28 oz)	crushed tomatoes
2 tbsp	tomato paste
1	bay leaf
¾ lb	lean ground beef
1	egg, beaten
¼ cup	water
1 tsp	chili powder
½ tsp	ground cumin
	salt and freshly ground pepper, to taste
½ cup	small pasta shells

1 Place the beans in a medium saucepan. Add cold water to cover and let soak overnight. Boil the beans to a boil for 10 minutes, drain and discard the water.

2 In a large saucepan, combine the beans and broth. Bring to a boil over high heat. Skim the surface. Add the carrots, onions, garlic, tomatoes, tomato paste and bay leaf. Lower the heat, cover and let simmer for 1 hour, until the beans are tender.

3 In a bowl, mix the ground beef, egg, water, chili powder and cumin together, and season with salt and pepper. Form the mixture into small balls and add to the soup. Let simmer for 20 minutes.

4 Add the pasta shells and cook for another 10 minutes, or until the pasta is tender. Serve piping hot.

Traditional Soups

Pea Soup

4 SERVINGS

½ **cup**	green split peas
2 tbsp	butter
1	onion, chopped
2	celery stalks, thinly sliced
2	carrots, peeled and cubed
	salt and freshly ground pepper, to taste
1	bay leaf
1 tsp	dried basil
1 tsp	dried oregano
1 tsp	dried thyme
2 cups	chicken broth
½ **cup**	slivered cooked ham or Canadian bacon

1 Sort and rinse the split peas.

2 In a large heavy saucepan, melt the butter over medium heat. Add the onion and cook, stirring often, until tender. Add the remaining vegetables, and cook, stirring often for 10 minutes, until softened. Season with salt and pepper and add the herbs.

3 Add the chicken broth, the peas and the ham. Bring to a boil. Lower the heat, cover and simmer for approximately 2 hours or until the soup becomes almost a purée in texture.

4 Taste for seasoning, and remove the bay leaf. Serve piping hot.

Traditional Soups

Cantonese Tofu Soup

4 SERVINGS

2 tbsp	vegetable oil
1	onion, sliced
1	garlic clove, chopped
1 tbsp	peeled, chopped fresh ginger
5 oz	boneless pork chops, cut in thin strips
5 oz	firm tofu, julienned
4 cups	chicken broth
½ cup	julienned bamboo shoots
1 cup	shredded spinach
1	tomato, seeded, julienned
	salt and freshly ground pepper, to taste
1 tsp	sugar
2 tbsp	cornstarch, mixed with 3 tbsp cold water
1	bunch of green onions, chopped

1 Heat the oil in a wok or a large skillet and brown the onion, garlic and ginger. Add the pork and the tofu, and stir-fry unti the pork just loses its pink color.

2 Meanwhile, pour the chicken broth into a medium saucepan and bring to a boil over high heat. Remove from the heat. Add the bamboo shoots, spinach and tomato to the wok. Lower the heat.

3 Add the hot chicken broth to the wok and cook for approximately 5 minutes, until the pork is tender. Season with salt and pepper and add the sugar.

4 Stir in the cornstarch mixture and cook, stirring, until the soup is thickened. Taste for seasoning. Serve sprinkled with the chopped green onions.

Traditional Soups

Avgolomono
Lemon-rice Soup

4 SERVINGS

4 cups	chicken broth
⅓ cup	rice
2	eggs
	grated zest and juice of 1 lemon
	salt and freshly ground pepper, to taste
¼ cup	chopped fresh parsley

1 In a heavy medium saucepan, bring the chicken broth to a boil over high heat.

2 Add the rice, lower the heat, cover and let simmer for approximately 15 minutes or until the rice is tender.

3 In a small bowl, whisk the eggs with the lemon juice; season with salt and pepper. Whisk in a bit of the hot broth to warm them, then transfer to the soup, whisking well. Remove from the heat.

4 Serve immediately, sprinkled with the fresh parsley and the lemon zest.

Note

To prepare this soup in advance, stop preparations at stage #3, beating the eggs, but do not add to the soup. This step must be done just before serving.

Traditional Soups

Cabbage Soup

6 SERVINGS

4 tbsp	butter
1	onion, chopped
2	garlic cloves, chopped
3 cups	sliced cabbage
2	celery stalks, thinly sliced
2	carrots, peeled, thinly sliced
	salt and freshly ground pepper, to taste
1	bay leaf
1 tsp	dried oregano
1 tsp	dried thyme
4 cups	beef broth
	rosemary sprigs (garnish)

1 In a large heavy saucepan, melt the butter over medium-low heat. Add the onion and garlic, and cook, stirring often, until tender.

2 Add the remaining vegetables, and cook, stirring often, for 5 to 10 minutes, until slightly softened. Season and add the herbs.

3 Add the beef broth, increase the heat and bring to a boil. Lower the heat, cover and let simmer for 40 to 45 minutes, until the soup is very flavorful.

4 Taste for seasoning and remove the bay leaf. Serve piping hot, garnished with rosemary sprigs.

Note

A piece of smoked pork may be added at the beginning of cooking and removed at the very end; bits of crisp fried bacon may also be added to the soup.

French Onion Soup

4 SERVINGS

4 tbsp	butter
2	onions, thinly sliced
½ cup	dry red wine
4 cups	beef broth
	salt and freshly ground pepper, to taste
4	slices of crusty bread, toasted
1 cup	grated gruyère or swiss cheese

1 In a large heavy saucepan, melt the butter over medium heat. Add the onions and cook, stirring often, for approximately 10 minutes, or until they are soft and golden.

2 Deglaze with the red wine and add the beef broth. Bring to a boil. Lower the heat and let simmer for 20 to 30 minutes, until richly flavored. Season to taste with salt and pepper.

3 Meanwhile, preheat the oven to 350° F. Place the bread slices on a baking sheet, sprinkle with the cheese and bake until melted and bubbly.

4 Taste for seasoning. To serve, fill each bowl with the soup and top with a cheese toast.

Traditional Soups

Strawberry and Tarragon Soup

4 SERVINGS

3 cups	fresh strawberries, hulled
1 cup	orange juice
	grated zest and juice of 1 lemon
	honey, to taste
1 to 2 tbsp	chopped fresh tarragon
	freshly ground pepper, to taste
	small tarragon bouquets (garnish)

1 Set aside the 4 nicest whole strawberries for the garnish. Place the remaining strawberries in a food processor and chop fine. Do not purée.

2 Place the strawberries in a medium bowl and add the orange juice and lemon juice.

3 Sweeten to taste with the honey and add the lemon zest and the tarragon, to taste. Season with pepper.

4 Cover and chill until ready to serve. Garnish each bowl with a strawberry cut in a fan shape and a small bouquet of tarragon.

Dessert Soups

Winter Fruit Soup

4 SERVINGS

2½ cups water	
¼ cup	honey
1 tbsp	peeled and finely chopped fresh ginger
	grated zest and juice of 1 lemon
1	cinnamon stick
½ cup	dried apricot halves
½ cup	halved dried plums
½ cup	halved pitted dates
½ cup	halved figs
½ cup	raisins

1 In a heavy medium nonaluminum saucepan, combine all ingredients and bring to a boil over medium heat.

2 Lower the heat. Cover and let simmer for 10 minutes, until the fruit has softened.

3 Remove from the heat and let stand to cool. Cover and refrigerate until ready to serve. Remove the cinnamon stick.

4 Serve chilled or warm by reheating briefly, accompanied with vanilla ice cream, if you like.

Note

Even if you do not like dried fruit, this dessert will seduce you, because fruit prepared in this manner become tender and juicy.

Dessert Soups

Blueberry
and Brown Sugar Soup

4 SERVINGS

2 cups	milk
1 tbsp	cornstarch mixed with 2 tbsp cold water
½ tsp	vanilla extract
2 cups	fresh blueberries
¼ cup	firmly packed light brown sugar

1 In a heavy medium nonaluminum saucepan, heat the milk to the boiling point over medium heat. Lower the heat slightly.

2 Add the cornstarch mixture and cook, whisking the milk vigorously until it thickens slightly. Add another 1 tsp of cornstarch (mixed with 1 tbsp cold water)if needed.

3 Remove from the heat. Add the vanilla extract and ladle the mixture into large soup bowls to cover the bottom.

4 Arrange the blueberries in a delicate fashion over the soup and sprinkle with the brown sugar. Serve immediately.

Note

You can reverse the presentation steps for this soup; first place the blueberries in the bowls, sprinkle with the brown sugar, and then coat with the sauce.

Dessert Soups

Red Fruit and Honey Soup

4 SERVINGS

1 cup	hulled and quartered fresh strawberries
1 cup	fresh raspberries
1 cup	halved and pitted fresh bing cherries
2 cups	cranberry juice
¼ cup	honey
½ tsp	ground cinnamon
1 tbsp	chopped fresh mint
4	honeycomb wafers (optional)
4	small sprigs of fresh mint (garnish)

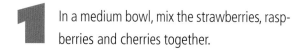

1. In a medium bowl, mix the strawberries, raspberries and cherries together.

2. In a small bowl, mix the cranberry juice, honey, chopped mint and cinnamon together.

3. Pour the juice mixture over the fruit. Cover and let steep for 1 hour in the refrigerator.

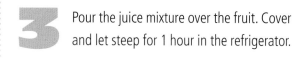

4. Serve the fruit soup in dessert cups, garnished with a honeycomb wafer, if desired, and a sprig of fresh mint.

Note

Strawberries and raspberries are very fragile and perishable; they should only be washed just before using them.

Dessert Soups

Cream of Chestnut 'n' Chocolate

4 SERVINGS

½ cup	canned unsweetened chestnut purée
¾ cup	light cream
¼ cup	confectioners' sugar
1 tbsp	unsweetened cocoa powder
½ cup	milk
1 tsp	vanilla extract
	finely chopped milk or semisweet chocolate

1 Place the chestnut purée in a food processor. Gradually add the cream while processing.

2 In a medium bowl, combine the confectioners' sugar and the cocoa. Gradually whisk in the milk. Add the vanilla.

3 Pour the milk mixture into the chestnut mixture, and process until smooth and a little frothy.

4 Taste for sweetness and thin with a bit of milk as required. Fill 4 dessert or coffee cups with the soup and garnish each with the chocolate. Refrigerate until ready to serve.

Dessert Soups

Cherry and Kirsch Soup

4 SERVINGS

1 can (19 oz)	bing cherries, with juice
½ cup	plain yogurt
¾ cup	milk
	granulated sugar, to taste
3 tbsp	kirsch
¼ cup	heavy cream
2 tsp	confectioners' sugar

1 Set aside a dozen whole cherries. Drain the remaining cherries and set aside the juice. Place the drained cherries in a food processor, and process while gradually adding the milk, yogurt and reserved cherry juice.

2 Sweeten to taste with granulated sugar. Add the kirsch. Process until the mixture is smooth. Transfer to a bowl and refrigerate until ready to serve.

3 Whip the cream and confectioners' sugar in a small bowl until stiff.

4 Taste the soup for sweetness and thin with a little milk if necessary. Fill 4 small bowls with the soup and garnish with a dollop of whipped cream and the whole cherries.

Dessert Soups

Sparkling Berry Soup

4 SERVINGS

¼ **cup**	orange liqueur (Grand Marnier, Cointreau, etc.)
3 tbsp	grenadine syrup
2 cups	mixed fresh berries (raspberries, blueberries, blackberries, etc.)
4 tsp	confectioners' sugar
1	bottle of favorite sparkling wine, cold

1 Mix the orange liqueur with the grenadine in a cup. Set aside.

2 Divide the berries among 4 dessert bowls or goblets and sprinkle each with the 1 teaspoon confectioners' sugar.

3 Pour the liqueur and syrup mixture evenly over the fruit. Refrigerate until ready to serve.

4 Just before serving, fill the dessert bowls or goblets with the cold sparkling wine and enjoy immediately, before the wine loses all its bubbles.

Dessert Soups

Index

A
Asparagus
   Velouté 119
   Vietnamese Soup 159
Autumn Soup 67
Avgolomono Lemon-rice Soup 167
Avocado
   Chilled Soup 19
   Cream 79
   Soup 53

B
Barley
   Cream 105
Basil
   Cream of Tomato Express 75
Beet
   Cream 83
Beef and Cabbage Soup 27
Beer Soup 61
Berry
   Sparkling Soup 185
Black Bean Soup 153
Blueberry and Brown Sugar Soup 177
Bouillon
   Julienned Vegetable and Vermicelli 41
Broccoli Soup 37
Brown Sugar and Blueberry Soup 177

C
Cabbage
   and Beef Soup 27
   Soup 169
Cantonese Tofu Soup 165
Carrot and Lemon Grass Velouté 117

Cauliflower
   Chilled Velouté 9
Celery
   Cream 77
Cherry and Kirsch Soup 183
Chervil and Watercress Velouté 129
Chestnut 'n' Chocolate
   Cream 181
Chick Pea Surprise 25
Chicken
   Fiesta Soup 45
Chilled Algerian Soup 15
Chilled Avocado Soup 19
Chilled Cauliflower Velouté 9
Chilled Melon Soup 11
Chilled Yogurt and Fennel Soup 13
Chinese Noodle Soup 145
Chocolate 'n' Chestnut
   Cream 181
Chowder
   Clam 43
   Corn 155
   Seafood and Clam 147
Clam
   Classic Chowder 43
   Seafood Chowder 147
Classic Clam Chowder 43
Coriander
Cream of Papaya 139
Corn and Vegetable Soup 59
Corn Chowder 155
Country Velouté 133
Cream
   of Avocado 79
   of Barley 105
   of Beet 83

of Celery 77
of Chestnut 'n' Chocolate 181
of Endive 95
of Fennel and Cucumber 115
of Fennel and Snow Crab 111
of Leek and Smoked Oysters 55
of Mixed Greens 125
of Mushroom 91
of Mussels with Saffron 89
of Onion 93
of Papaya and Coriander 139
of Poultry and Lettuce 131
of Spinach with Peaches 123
of Squash and Pepper with Maple Syrup 113
of Tomato Florentine 107
of Tomato and Basil Express 75
of Watercress 99
Cucumber
    Cream of Fennel 115

E
Endive
    Cream 95
Exotic Broccoli Soup 37

F
Fennel
    Chilled Yogurt Soup 13
    Cream of Cucumber 115
    Cream of Snow Crab 111
Fiesta Chicken Soup 45
Five-Season Soup (Shi jin tàng) 149
Flemish Soup 97
Floating Avocado Soup 53
French Onion Soup 171

G
Garlic Soup 69
Gazpacho 17
Green Onion
    Potage Parmentier 85
Gruyère Soup 49

H
Ham and Lentil Soup 47
Hearty Seafood Potage 65
Honey and Red Fruit Soup 179

I
Irish Soup 141
Italian Vegetable Soup (Minestrone) 35

J
Julienned Vegetable and Vermicelli Bouillon 41

K
Kirsch and Cherry Soup 183

L
Leek
    Cream of Smoked Oysters 55
Leek Velouté 87
Lemon Grass and Carrot Velouté 117
Lemon-rice
    Avgolomono Soup 167
Lentil
    and Ham Soup 47
    and Spinach Soup 23
Lettuce
    Cream of Poultry 131

M
Maple Syrup
    Cream of Squash and Pepper 113
Melon
    Chilled Soup 11
Mexican Soup (Sopa De Hambre Gringo) 161
Minestrone 35
    alla Casalinga 143
Mint-flavoured Mushroom and Escargot Velouté 109
Mixed Greens
    Cream 125
Mushroom
    Cream 91
    and Escargot Velouté 109

Mussels
  Cream with Saffron 89

N
Noodle
  Chinese Soup 145

O
Onion
  Cream 93
  Soup 171
Orange
  Potage Crécy 127
Orchard Soup 73

P
Papaya
  Cream of Coriander 139
Pea Soup 163
Peaches
  Cream of Spinach 123
Pepper
  Cream of Squash with Maple Syrup 113
Pistou 21
Potage
  Crécy à l'Orange 127
  Grenoblois 121
  Hearty Seafood 65
  Parmentier with Green Onion 85
Poultry
  Cream of Lettuce 131
  Rice Soup 33
Pumpkin
  Thai Soup 71

R
Red Fruit and Honey Soup 179
Red Pepper Velouté 137
Red Wine Soup 57
Rice Soup
  Poultry 33
  Vegetable Soup 39

Rutabaga Velouté 101

S
Saffron
  Cream of Mussels 89
Seafood
  Hearty Potage 65
Seafood and Clam Chowder 147
Shrimp
  Spicy Soup 151
Smoked Oysters
  Cream of Leek 55
Smoked Salmon Velouté à la Vichy 135
Snow Crab
  Cream of Fennel 111
Soup
  Autumn 67
  Avgolomono Lemon-rice 167
  Beef and Cabbage 27
  Beer 61
  Berry 185
  Black Bean 153
  Blueberry and Brown Sugar 177
  Cabbage 169
  Cantonese Tofu 165
  Cherry and Kirsch 183
  Chilled Algerian 15
  Chilled Avocado 19
  Chilled Melon 11
  Chilled Yogurt and Fennel 13
  Chinese Noodle 145
  Corn and Vegetable 59
  Exotic Broccoli 37
  Fiesta Chicken 45
  Five-Season (Shi jin tàng) 149
  Flemish 97
  Floating Avocado 53
  French Onion 171
  Garlic 69
  Gruyère 49
  Ham and Lentil 47
  Irish 141

Italian Vegetable (Minestrone) 35
Mexican (Sopa De Hambre Gringo) 161
Orchard 73
Pea 163
Poultry Rice 33
Red Fruit and Honey 179
Red Wine 57
Royale 29
Spiced 63
Spicy Shrimp 151
Spinach and Lentil 23
Spinach 81
Strawberry and Tarragon 173
Thai Pumpkin 71
Vegetable 51
Vegetable Rice 39
Vietnamese Asparagus 159
Winter Fruit 175
Won Ton 157
Yogurt 7
Soupe à la Bonne Femme 31
Spinach
    and Lentil Soup 23
    Cream with Peaches 123
    Soup 81
Squash
    Cream of Pepper with Maple Syrup 113
Strawberry and Tarragon Soup 173

T
Tarragon
    and Strawberry Soup 173
Thai Pumpkin Soup 71
Tofu
    Cantonese Soup 165
Tomato
    Cream Florentine 107
    Cream of Basil Express 75

V
Vegetable
    and Corn Soup 59
    and Vermicelli Bouillon 41
    Italian Soup (Minestrone) 35
    Rice Soup 39
    Soup 51
Velouté
    Asparagus 119
    Chilled Cauliflower 9
    Country 133
    Leek 87
    Lemon Grass and Carrot 117
    Milanaise 103
    Mint-flavoured Mushroom and Escargot 109
    Red Pepper 137
    Rutabaga 101
    Smoked Salmon 135
    Watercress and Chervil 129
Vermicelli
    and Julienned Vegetable Bouillon 41
Vietnamese Asparagus Soup 159

W
Watercress
    and Chervil Velouté 129
    Cream 99
Winter Fruit Soup 175
Won Ton Soup 157

Y
Yogurt
    Chilled and Fennel Soup 13
    Soup 7

Notes